INSPIRED TO ENCOURAGE

EXPLORING ENCOURAGEMENT IN CHRISTIAN COMMUNITY

*To my dearest Ellie Gustafson—
Your life is a masterclass in the art of encouragement. With a heart always ready to uplift, you have taught me the invaluable lesson of noticing the often overlooked whispers of kindness and support. Your unwavering presence and the gentle strength of your encouragement have been a beacon in my faith journey. Truly, you are a blessing beyond measure, embodying the very essence of what it means to uplift and inspire. Thank you for being my steadfast encourager and a remarkable blessing in my life.*

Tio Felipe
DESIGNS

tiofelipe.com

amazon.com/author/tiofelipe

First published by Tio Felipe Designs 2024
https://www.tiofelipe.com/

Copyright © February 2024 by Tio Felipe

All rights reserved. No part of this publication may be reproduced, stored or transmitted in any form or by any means, electronic, mechanical, photocopying, recording, scanning, or otherwise without written permission from the publisher. It is illegal to copy this book, post it to a website, or distribute it by any other means without permission.

First edition

Dear Reader,

Thank you for choosing this book! If you enjoyed it, we kindly ask you to take a moment and share your thoughts by writing a review on Amazon. Your feedback helps us improve and reach more readers.

We appreciate your support and look forward to hearing about your experience with the book.

Happy reading!

Tio Felipe
www.amazon.com/author/tiofelipe

INSPIRED TO ENCOURAGE

EXPLORING ENCOURAGEMENT IN CHRISTIAN COMMUNITY

Contents

Introduction	1
Chapter 1: The Foundations of Encouragement	3
Chapter 2: The Art of Saying No Positively	9
Chapter 3: Building Bridges Through Encouragement	13
Chapter 4: The Encouragement of Community	17
Chapter 5: The Power of Words	21
Chapter 6: The Practice of Gratitude as Encouragement	25
Chapter 7: Reflection as a Tool for Encouragement	29
Chapter 8: Encouragement in Leadership	33
Conclusion: Cultivating a Legacy of Encouragement	37
Works Cited	39
Appendices	41
Discussion Questions for Reflection or Small Groups	42
Living in Community: "One Another" Passages	44
30-Day Encouragement Challenge	48
Scripture Reference Guide for Encouragement	53
Guide to Active Listening	55
Prayer Guide for Encouragement	58
Incorporating Encouragement into Daily Life	62
Inventory of Spiritual Gifts	64
Echoes of Grace Poem	67

"Do not waste time bothering whether you 'love' your neighbor; act as if you did. As soon as we do this we find one of the great secrets. When you are behaving as if you loved someone, you will presently come to love him."

—C.S. Lewis, Mere Christianity

Introduction

In the three and a half decades that I have walked the path of Christian ministry, I have been privileged to witness the transformative power of encouragement in the lives of individuals and communities. From the lecture halls of Christian Higher Education to the dynamic fields of mission work and within the sacred spaces of local church pastoral care, my journey has been marked by diverse experiences that have deepened my understanding of and passion for spiritual growth. As a current Executive Pastor, I reflect on the myriad ways encouragement has been a tool for ministry and a cornerstone of my spiritual practice.

This book is born out of a deeply held conviction that the art of encouragement is the heart of spiritual growth. This conviction has been nurtured over years of serving, learning, and leading in various capacities within the Christian community. My passion for helping others grow spiritually through knowing God's Word, reflection, practicing gratitude, and encouraging others is the foundation upon which these pages are built. I believe that encouragement is not merely a nice-to-have aspect of Christian life but an essential, life-giving practice that echoes the teachings of Scripture and the example of Christ Himself.

The journey of writing this book is an invitation to explore the multifaceted nature of encouragement. Through the lens of my experiences and the wisdom distilled from critical texts on the subject, we will delve into how encouragement operates as a powerful mechanism for spiritual deepening, relational building, and community strengthening. From understanding the biblical mandate to "encourage one another" to mastering the art of positive refusal, building bridges through simple acts of kindness, fostering an encouraging community, and leveraging the power of words to uplift and heal—this book aims to equip you with the insights and tools necessary for cultivating a practice of encouragement that transforms lives.

As we embark on this journey together, I hope you will find, within these pages, not only practical guidance and inspiration but also a reflection of the heart of God. A heart that calls each of us to be bearers of encouragement, to speak life into the dry places, to uplift the weary soul, and to illuminate the path for others with the light of His love and grace. This is the journey of encouragement we are invited to walk—a journey that reshapes our world, one word, one act, one heart at a time.

Chapter 1
The Foundations of Encouragement

Encouragement is the very breath of the church, a divine whisper that sustains, uplifts, and propels us forward. It is more than a gentle pat on the back or a fleeting word of comfort; encouragement is a commandment deeply rooted in the fabric of Scripture, calling us to act as conduits of God's love and compassion. This chapter lays the foundation for understanding the biblical imperative of encouragement, exploring its significance in the believer's life and the transformative impact it can have within the Christian community.

The Biblical Command to Encourage

The call to encourage one another is woven throughout the Scriptures, serving as a divine directive for how we interact within the body of Christ. Hebrews 3:13 exhorts us to "encourage one another daily," a command highlighting the ongoing necessity of encouragement in our daily walk with God and each other. Similarly, 1 Thessalonians 5:11 instructs us to "encourage one another and build each other up," pointing to encouragement as a critical component of spiritual growth and communal strength. These passages, among others, underscore the understanding that encouragement is not optional; it is a vital practice mandated by God to nurture faith and strengthen bonds within the Christian fellowship.

The Theological Underpinnings of Encouragement

At its core, encouragement is an expression of love and grace that reflects the heart of God towards His creation. It is a manifestation of the "one another" commands central to Christian ethics, embodying the principles of mutual care, support, and edification. Encouragement is grounded in the theological truth that we are created for community, designed to live in relationship with God and one another. As such, it serves as a tangible expression of the interconnectedness of the body of Christ, where each member plays a crucial role in the spiritual well-being of the whole.

The Role of Encouragement in Spiritual Growth

Encouragement is a catalyst for spiritual growth for the individual and the community. It has the power to uplift the downtrodden, strengthen the weak, and restore hope to the despairing. By pointing others to the truths of Scripture, offering timely words of comfort, and affirming God's promises, we participate in the work of spiritual formation. Encouragement helps to cultivate an environment where faith can flourish, doubts can be openly addressed, and individuals are motivated to pursue deeper intimacy with God.

The Transformative Impact of Encouragement

The impact of encouragement extends beyond the immediate moment of exchange; it can potentially effect lasting change in the lives of individuals and the community. Encouragement nurtures resilience, fosters perseverance, and inspires faithfulness in the face of challenges. It also acts as a bridge, connecting hearts and minds in a shared experience of God's grace. When we encourage one another, we are essentially participating in God's transformative work, enabling others to see themselves and their circumstances through the lens of God's redemptive plan.

Practical Ways to Cultivate Encouragement

Encouraging one another involves both words and actions. It can be as simple as sending a note of appreciation, offering a listening ear, or sharing a Scripture verse that speaks to someone's situation. It also involves being present, bearing one another's burdens, and celebrating each other's victories. To cultivate a practice of encouragement, we must intentionally seek opportunities to uplift others, stay attuned to the needs of those around us, and allow the Holy Spirit to guide our interactions.

The foundation of encouragement is built upon the understanding that it is a divine mandate rooted in the nature of God and central to the church's life. As we explore the depths of this calling, let us be inspired to embrace the practice of encouragement with renewed vigor, recognizing its power to transform lives and strengthen the bonds of Christian fellowship. Encouragement is not just a duty; it is a privilege—a means through which we can reflect the love and grace of God to a world in desperate need of hope.

Chapter 2
The Art of Saying No Positively

In our journey of encouragement, we often face the challenge of balancing our desire to uplift others with the necessity of setting healthy boundaries. The art of saying "no" positively and constructively is not just about self-preservation; it's vital to encourage others and us. This chapter explores the concept of the positive "no," adapted from William Ury's principles, and how it can be a powerful tool for encouragement within a Christian framework.

Understanding the Positive "No"

A positive "no" fundamentally affirms our values, priorities, and God-given purpose. It's a declaration that, while we might be unable to fulfill a specific request, our commitment to God's will and our ministry remains unwavering. This form of "no" is not a rejection but a redirection of our energies to what we truly believe God is calling us to do. It requires discernment, wisdom, and a deep understanding of our limitations and capacities as stewards of God's gifts.

The Biblical Basis for Boundaries

Scripture provides ample evidence of the importance of boundaries, showing us that even Jesus set limits to His availability and chose where to direct His energies (Mark 1:35-38). The apostle Paul also teaches us to let our "yes" be yes and our "no" be no (James 5:12), emphasizing the importance of clear and honest communication. By setting boundaries, we practice good stewardship of our time and resources and model a biblical approach to personal integrity and respect for others.

The Role of "No" in Encouragement

Saying "no" can be an act of encouragement. When we set boundaries, we offer others a model of healthy Christian living, demonstrating how to prioritize God's calling and personal well-being. It also opens opportunities for others to step in and use their gifts, fostering a more diverse and active community where everyone contributes according to their abilities. In this way, a positive "no" can encourage growth, independence, and a deeper reliance on God within the body of Christ.

Practical Steps for Saying "No" Positively

1. **Pray for Wisdom**: Before responding to requests, seek God's guidance to understand His will and the best course of action.
2. **Affirm the Relationship**: Begin your response by affirming your care and respect for the person or the importance of the request.
3. **State Your "No" Clearly**: Straightforwardly communicate your decision, avoiding ambiguity.
4. **Explain Briefly**: Briefly explain your commitment to God's calling and your current responsibilities without feeling compelled to over-justify.
5. **Offer an Alternative**: Suggest an alternative solution or person who can meet the need.

Encouraging Others Through Our "No"

Our ability to say "no" positively can encourage others by setting an example of balanced Christian living. It shows that we are committed to following God's leading, even when it means making tough choices. This can inspire others to consider their boundaries and commitments, leading to healthier relationships and a stronger faith community.

The art of saying "no" positively is an essential skill in the Christian life, enabling us to encourage others by modeling healthy boundaries and priorities. As we navigate the demands of ministry and daily life, let us seek to embody this practice with grace and wisdom, trusting that our "no" can be just as powerful an act of encouragement as our "yes." Through this balance, we can better serve God, fulfill our calling, and uplift those around us in a manner that honors Him and builds up the body of Christ.

Chapter 3
Building Bridges Through Encouragement

One of the most profound ways to encourage others in their faith and life journey is through genuine, heartfelt connections. Drawing inspiration from Bill Hybels' "Just Walk Across the Room," this chapter explores how simple steps of kindness and open, meaningful conversations can become influential acts of encouragement. By reaching out, we build bridges between hearts and foster an environment where faith can flourish.

The Power of Presence

The simple act of being present can speak volumes to those around us. In a world increasingly filled with distractions and digital interactions, the intentional choice to be fully present with someone is a rare and precious form of encouragement. It signals to the other person that they are valued and worthy of our time and attention. As Christians, our presence can be a testament to the love and care of Jesus, who always made time to engage deeply with individuals, from His disciples to the crowds who sought Him.

Conversations as a Gateway

Engaging in meaningful conversations is an art that requires patience, listening, and empathy. When we initiate discussions with an open heart and a genuine interest in the other person, we create a safe space for sharing and exploration. These conversations can become gateways to deeper understanding, spiritual insights, and mutual encouragement. They allow us to share our faith experiences in a natural and non-threatening way, inviting others to reflect on their beliefs and relationship with God.

Practical Tips for Encouraging Conversations

1. **Listen More Than You Speak**: Show genuine interest in the other person's story, beliefs, and feelings. Listening is a powerful form of encouragement that validates the other's experience.

2. **Ask Open-Ended Questions**: Encourage dialogue by asking questions that require more than a yes or no answer. This invites deeper reflection and conversation.

3. **Share Your Journey**: When appropriate, share your own experiences of faith and how God has worked in your life. Be honest about your struggles and victories, as this can encourage others to see how God moves in various circumstances.

4. **Offer Encouragement Through Scripture**: When it feels right, share relevant Scripture that has been meaningful to you. This can provide comfort, guidance, and a new perspective to those seeking answers.

5. **Pray Together**: If the moment arises, offer to pray with the person. Prayer can be a decisive moment of connection and encouragement, reminding both of you of God's presence and love.

Building Bridges in Everyday Encounters

Encouragement doesn't require grand gestures; it can be woven into the fabric of our daily lives through simple acts of kindness and openness. Whether it's a smile, a thoughtful word, or taking the time to ask someone how they're genuinely doing, these small actions can build bridges of encouragement. By being intentional in our interactions, we can reflect Christ's love and compassion in tangible ways that draw others closer to Him.

The Impact of Encouragement on Community

When individuals feel encouraged, they are more likely to

engage with and contribute to their community. Encouragement fosters a positive environment where people feel supported and valued, leading to more robust, cohesive faith communities. As we practice building bridges through encouragement, we strengthen individual faith journeys and foster a collective spirit of love, support, and growth within the body of Christ.

Building bridges through encouragement is a calling that reflects the heart of Jesus' ministry. By being present, engaging in meaningful conversations, and practicing simple acts of kindness, we can encourage others in ways that have eternal significance. As we walk this path, let us be mindful of the opportunities God places before us to uplift and strengthen the faith of those around us, building bridges that lead to deeper connections and a more vibrant community of believers.

Chapter 4
The Encouragement of Community

Dietrich Bonhoeffer's seminal work, "Life Together," provides profound insights into the essence and importance of Christian community. This chapter draws on Bonhoeffer's wisdom and personal ministry experiences to explore how living in community acts as a source of mutual encouragement and spiritual growth. The Christian community is not just a gathering of individuals; it is a dynamic, living body where each member plays a crucial role in encouraging and building one another.

The Spiritual Value of Community

The New Testament is replete with metaphors and teachings emphasizing the church as a body of believers united in Christ. This unity is not merely theoretical but practical and lived out in everyday interactions. In community, we find a tangible expression of God's love and grace, a place where we can bear one another's burdens (Galatians 6:2) and encourage one another towards love and good deeds (Hebrews 10:24-25). The spiritual value of community lies in its reflection of the triune God—a God of relationship, fellowship, and mutual indwelling.

Practices for Fostering an Encouraging Community

1. **Shared Worship and Prayer**: Gathering regularly for worship and prayer is the heartbeat of Christian community. These acts of devotion orient the community around Christ, fostering a sense of unity and mutual encouragement.

2. **Studying Scripture Together**: Engaging with God's

Exploring Encouragement in Christian Community

Word in a communal setting allows for diverse insights and encourages members to grow in understanding and faith. Through the shared exploration of Scripture, individuals are encouraged in their walk with God and their relationships with one another.

3. **Practicing Hospitality**: Opening our homes and lives to one another is a powerful encouragement. Hospitality creates spaces for deeper relationships to form and for the community to practice the "one another" commands of Scripture in real and tangible ways.

4. **Serving Together**: Engaging in service projects or mission work as a community not only meets the needs of others but also strengthens the bonds within the community itself. Serving together encourages an outward-focused vision, a sense of purpose, and camaraderie among members.

The Role of Listening and Speaking in Community

In a healthy community, listening and speaking are infused with the desire to encourage and edify. Listening attentively to one another is an act of love that affirms the value of each member. Speaking, on the other hand, should always aim to build up, not tear down—sharing words of comfort, encouragement, and truth in love (Ephesians 4:29). The dynamic interplay between listening and speaking helps maintain the health and vibrancy of the community.

The Impact of Encouragement on Individual and Community Growth

The encouragement found within Christian community has a compounding effect. It nurtures the individual's faith and well-being and strengthens the community's collective witness to the world. A community characterized by encouragement is a beacon of hope, a place where people are drawn to experience the love and grace of Christ firsthand. As members of such a community, we are continually reminded that we are not alone in our faith journey. Together, we can face challenges, celebrate victories, and grow more deeply in our relationship with God.

The encouragement of community is foundational to the Christian life. As we strive to live out the principles of "Life Together" and embody the teachings of Scripture, we create an environment where encouragement flourishes. By prioritizing worship, prayer, Scripture study, hospitality, and service, we cultivate a community that supports and uplifts its members and extends a welcoming hand to those outside its boundaries. In doing so, we witness the transformative power of living in community—a power rooted in the mutual encouragement and love that reflect the heart of the gospel.

Chapter 5
The Power of Words

Drawing from the insights of Brady Boyd's "Speaking Life: Words That Work Wonders," this chapter explores the profound impact our words can have on encouragement and spiritual growth. The Bible teaches us that life and death are in the power of the tongue (Proverbs 18:21), highlighting the significant role our speech plays in building up or tearing down those around us. In this chapter, we delve into how to harness the power of words to encourage, uplift, and bring life to our communities and relationships.

Understanding the Impact of Our Words

Our words are a reflection of our hearts (Luke 6:45). They have the potential to inspire hope, instill courage, and affirm the value of others, but they can also cause hurt, sow seeds of doubt, and undermine the work of encouragement. Recognizing the weight of our words is the first step in learning to use them as tools for building up the body of Christ. We are called to be stewards of our speech, carefully choosing words that reflect God's grace and love.

Biblical Principles for Encouraging Speech

The Scriptures provide clear guidance on how our speech should be characterized:
- **Edifying**: Our words should build up others, contributing to their growth and spiritual well-being (Ephesians 4:29).
- **Gracious**: Our speech should be seasoned with grace, making it appealing and beneficial to those who hear (Colossians 4:6).

Exploring Encouragement in Christian Community

- **Truthful**: Speaking the truth in love is essential for growth and maturity in the body of Christ (Ephesians 4:15).
- **Hopeful**: Our words should convey hope, pointing others to God's promises and faithfulness (Hebrews 10:23).

Practical Ways to Use Words for Encouragement

1. **Affirmation**: Regularly affirming others for their qualities, contributions, and efforts can bolster their confidence and sense of worth. Make it a habit to acknowledge and celebrate the strengths and achievements of those around you.

2. **Comfort**: In times of sorrow or difficulty, words of comfort can provide solace and reassurance. Sharing Scriptures that speak of God's presence and promises can be uplifting.

3. **Guidance**: Offering wise and timely advice grounded in biblical truth can steer someone toward God's path for their life. Be discerning and gentle, ensuring your words encourage rather than dictate.

4. **Prayer**: Praying with and for others is a powerful way to use words to encourage. It brings the person's needs before God and reminds them they are not alone in their struggles.

The Role of Listening in Encouraging Speech

Practical encouragement through words is not just about speaking but also listening. By actively listening to others, we gain insight into their needs, fears, and hopes, which allows us to tailor our encouragement to be more impactful. Listening demonstrates care and respect, laying the groundwork for words that genuinely speak life into someone's circumstances.

Navigating the Challenges of Digital Communication

In an age dominated by digital communication, the principles of encouraging speech extend to our online interactions. Social media, emails, and text messaging offer unique opportunities to encourage others beyond our immediate physical presence.

However, they also pose challenges, as tone and body language nuances are lost. Practice clarity, kindness, and intentionality in your digital communications to ensure they convey encouragement effectively.

The power of words to encourage and uplift cannot be overstated. As followers of Christ, we are called to harness this power responsibly, ensuring our speech reflects the gospel's love, grace, and truth. By committing to using our words to speak life, we can significantly impact our communities' spiritual health and growth, fostering environments where encouragement flourishes. Let us be mindful of the words we choose, always aiming to be bearers of hope, comfort, and encouragement in a world in desperate need of God's transforming love.

Chapter 6
The Practice of Gratitude as Encouragement

Gratitude is a powerful force in the Christian life, shaping our perspective, strengthening our faith, and influencing our interactions with others. This chapter explores how gratitude can serve as a foundational element of encouragement for us and those around us. By cultivating a grateful heart, we open the door to seeing God's hand at work in all circumstances, enabling us to be sources of encouragement grounded in God's goodness and faithfulness.

Gratitude in Scripture

The Bible is replete with exhortations to give thanks in all circumstances (1 Thessalonians 5:18), recognizing that every good gift comes from above (James 1:17). This acknowledgment of God's provision and care fosters a sense of gratitude that transcends our current situations, allowing us to maintain a posture of thankfulness even in trials. Gratitude in the Christian context is not just about being thankful for the good things but also about finding reasons to be thankful in the midst of challenges, seeing them as opportunities for growth and deeper reliance on God.

The Impact of Gratitude on Encouragement

Gratitude inherently encourages both the giver and receiver. When we express gratitude to others, we affirm their value and the significance of their actions, which can uplift and motivate them. Similarly, when we cultivate gratitude in our own lives, we are more likely to maintain a positive outlook, which is contagious and can inspire those around us. A grateful heart is more attuned to God's presence and activity, enabling us to encourage others from a place of genuine faith and trust in God's provisions.

Practical Ways to Practice Gratitude

1. **Daily Gratitude Journal**: Make a habit of recording three to five things you're thankful for each day. This practice helps to shift focus from problems to blessings, fostering a grateful heart.

2. **Gratitude in Prayer**: Incorporate thanksgiving into your daily prayers, specifically acknowledging God's hand at work in your life and the lives of others.

3. **Express Gratitude to Others**: Regularly communicate your appreciation to those around you—whether for specific acts of kindness, their presence in your life, or qualities you admire in them. This not only encourages them but also reinforces your sense of gratitude.

4. **Gratitude Visits or Letters**: Take the time to write a letter or visit someone to express gratitude for their impact on your life. This meaningful gesture can be incredibly encouraging to the recipient.

Encouraging Others Through Gratitude

Our expressions of gratitude can be a powerful form of encouragement to those around us. By recognizing and vocalizing how others have blessed us, we not only provide them with positive reinforcement but also remind them of the significance of their actions in God's larger tapestry. Encouraging others through gratitude involves seeing and acknowledging each individual's God-given value and contributions, fostering a community where appreciation and thankfulness are freely expressed.

The Role of Gratitude in Difficult Times

Gratitude is critical in navigating challenges, both personally and within our communities. It provides a lens through which we can see difficulties as opportunities for growth and trust in

God. Practicing gratitude in hard times can be an act of defiance against despair, a declaration that God is still good and faithful, which, in turn, encourages others to adopt a similar stance of faith and hope.

The practice of gratitude is a potent tool for encouragement, transforming our perspective and interactions to reflect God's goodness and grace. As we cultivate a lifestyle of thankfulness, we draw closer to God and become conduits of encouragement to those around us. Let us strive to be individuals and communities characterized by gratitude, recognizing the profound impact our thankfulness can have on encouraging ourselves and others towards deeper faith and joy in the Lord.

Chapter 7
Reflection as a Tool for Encouragement

Reflection is a powerful spiritual discipline that enables us to see God's hand in our lives, understand His Word more deeply, and recognize our growth and the areas where we need His grace. This chapter delves into how personal and communal reflection can be a significant tool for encouragement. By intentionally setting aside time to reflect on God's faithfulness, lessons learned, and the journey ahead, we cultivate a mindset that encourages ourselves and inspires others.

The Importance of Reflection in Spiritual Growth

Reflection is crucial for spiritual growth because it allows us to pause and consider our relationship with God and others. It helps us to digest experiences, see the bigger picture of God's work in our lives, and understand our responses from a spiritual perspective. Reflection turns experiences into insights, challenges into lessons, and questions into deeper faith. It encourages us by revealing how God has guided, protected, and loved us, even in ways we might not have initially seen.

Personal Reflection: A Daily Practice

Incorporating personal reflection into daily life can significantly enhance our spiritual well-being and capacity to encourage others. Here are some practical ways to engage in personal reflection:

1. **Scripture Reflection**: Start or end your day with a passage of Scripture, meditating on its meaning and application to

your life. Ask yourself what God is speaking to you through His Word.

2. **Examen**: Adopt the practice of Examen, a form of prayerful reflection from the Ignatian tradition. Review your day in the presence of God, noting moments of grace and areas for growth.

3. **Journaling**: Keep a spiritual journal to record prayers, insights, struggles, and moments of gratitude. Writing facilitates deeper processing and serves as a tangible reminder of God's presence and activity in your life.

Communal Reflection: Strengthening Bonds

Reflecting together as a community or small group strengthens relationships and fosters a supportive environment where encouragement flourishes. Sharing insights and experiences with others can provide affirmation, challenge, and deeper understanding. It highlights the collective journey of faith and how God works within the community.

1. **Shared Testimonies**: Regularly sharing personal testimonies within the group can be a powerful way to reflect on and celebrate God's faithfulness. It encourages the speaker and listeners by highlighting the transformative power of God's work.

2. **Group Bible Study and Reflection**: Engaging with Scripture as a group allows for a richer exploration of its application to life. It provides a space for mutual encouragement as members share different perspectives and insights.

The Encouraging Power of Reflective Listening

Active, reflective listening is an essential skill in encouraging others. We validate their feelings and provide support by truly hearing and seeking to understand another's experience. Reflective listening in pastoral care, mentoring, and everyday conversations encourages openness and vulnerability, creating deeper connections and fostering spiritual growth.

Reflection in Times of Difficulty

Reflection can be particularly encouraging in times of difficulty. It helps to put trials into perspective, reminding us of God's past faithfulness and His promises for the future. Reflecting on challenging times can reveal how they have contributed to our growth and prepared us for future ministry, encouraging us to trust God even in uncertainty.

Personal and communal reflection is vital for deepening our faith and encouraging others. It allows us to see more clearly, understand more deeply, and trust more fully. As we make reflection a regular part of our spiritual discipline, we become more attuned to God's work and better equipped to be sources of encouragement. Let us commit to reflection to draw nearer to God and each other, fostering a spirit of encouragement that radiates the hope and love of Christ.

Chapter 8
Encouragement in Leadership

Leadership within Christian ministry carries the unique opportunity and responsibility to be a source of encouragement to others. Drawing from 35 years of diverse ministry experiences, this chapter explores how leaders can embody and extend encouragement through their roles, whether in education, mission organizations, pastoral staff, or executive positions. Leadership is not merely about direction and decision-making; it's profoundly about inspiring, uplifting, and empowering those we serve.

The Essence of Encouraging Leadership

Encouraging leadership is rooted in the example of Christ, who led with compassion, empathy, and a deep commitment to nurturing His disciples and followers. It requires a leader to be both visionary and servant-hearted, capable of seeing the potential in others and dedicated to helping them grow into that potential. An encouraging leader fosters an environment where people feel valued, understood, and inspired to contribute their best.

Critical Practices of Encouraging Leaders

1. **Modeling Authenticity and Vulnerability**: Leaders encourage by example. Sharing your journey, including struggles and how you've seen God at work in your life, can deeply encourage others. It demonstrates that growth and strength often come through challenges.

2. **Affirming and Valuing Others**: Recognize and affirm the

unique contributions of each individual. Personalized encouragement can significantly impact someone's sense of worth and belonging.

3. **Fostering a Culture of Encouragement**: Create an environment where encouragement is a regular practice from leader to team and among all members. This might include regular times of sharing testimonies, celebrating achievements, and praying for one another.

4. **Investing in Individual Growth**: Take an active interest in the spiritual and professional development of those you lead. Offer mentorship, resources, and opportunities for growth tailored to the individual's needs and aspirations.

5. **Leading Through Listening**: Encouraging leaders are excellent listeners. They give others the space to share, dream, and express concerns, making them feel heard and supported.

Encouragement During Times of Change and Challenge

Leaders are often at the forefront during times of change and challenge. How they navigate these periods can be incredibly encouraging to others. Demonstrating trust in God, maintaining a positive outlook, and providing clear, compassionate communication can help guide and uplift those affected by uncertainty.

1. **Communicate with Clarity and Hope**: In times of change, clear communication that conveys hope and reassurance is vital. It helps mitigate fear and builds trust.

2. **Be Present and Accessible**: Being physically and emotionally present for your team or congregation during challenging times can offer significant encouragement. It reassures them they are not alone and their concerns are significant.

3. **Encourage Through Prayer**: Prayer seeks God's intervention and unites hearts and minds. Praying with and for your team or congregation during difficult times is a powerful act of leadership.

The Impact of Encouraging Leadership

Encouraging leadership has a ripple effect that extends far beyond immediate interactions. It cultivates a community characterized by faith, hope, and love. Encouraged individuals are likelier to step into their calling, contribute their gifts, and encourage others. Thus, the practice of encouraging leadership not only strengthens the fabric of the community but also amplifies its witness to the broader world.

Leadership in the Christian context is a calling to encourage, uplift, and empower. It's about guiding others in their journey of faith and service just as much as it is about directing organizational goals or pastoral care. By embodying the principles of encouraging leadership, we reflect the heart of Jesus and foster environments where individuals and communities can thrive in their God-given potential. Let us, as leaders, commit to being sources of encouragement, bearing witness to the transformative power of leading with love, empathy, and steadfast faith in God's promises.

Conclusion
Cultivating a Legacy of Encouragement

As we conclude this journey through the multifaceted landscape of encouragement in the Christian life, I hope these pages have served as a guide and a heartfelt invitation to cultivate a practice of encouragement deeply rooted in faith, hope, and love. Drawing from a rich tapestry of Scripture, personal ministry experience, and the wisdom of those who have walked the path of faith before us, we have explored the profound impact that encouragement can have on individuals, communities, and the world.

Encouragement is not merely an action but a way of being—a reflection of God's heart towards us, His beloved creation. In every word of comfort, every act of kindness, and every gesture of support, we echo the voice of the One who calls us by name and tells us we are loved. This is the essence of encouragement: to remind one another of the truth of who we are in Christ, especially in moments when we might have forgotten.

The journey of encouragement is both personal and communal. It begins in the quiet places of our hearts, in our daily walk with God, where we learn to listen to His voice and draw strength from His Word. It extends into our homes, workplaces, churches, and beyond—anywhere our lives touch the lives of others. As we practice gratitude, reflect, and use our words and actions to uplift, we become conduits of God's grace, impacting the world in ways we may never fully see this side of eternity.

For those of us called to lead, whether in pastoral roles, Christian education, missions, or any form of ministry, the call to encourage is also a call to model the humility, compassion, and servant-heartedness of Jesus. Leadership is an incredible platform for encouragement, offering unique opportunities to shape environments where people feel seen, known, and inspired to grow in their faith and calling.

As you move forward from this reading, I encourage you to see yourself as an integral part of God's plan to bring encouragement to a world in desperate need of hope. Whether through simple acts of kindness, words of affirmation, or the dedicated ministry of presence, your efforts to encourage others will bear fruit in ways you may never fully realize. Remember, the smallest seed of encouragement planted in faith can grow into a mighty tree whose branches offer shelter and rest to many.

May you be encouraged today by knowing that God is with you, equipping you, and delighting in your desire to serve Him through the ministry of encouragement. And as you pour out encouragement to others, may you be deeply replenished by the inexhaustible wellspring of God's love and grace.

Let us move forward in the strength of the Lord, committed to cultivating a legacy of encouragement that echoes through generations, drawing hearts closer to the One who is our greatest Encourager.

Works Cited

Bonhoeffer, Dietrich. Life Together: The Classic Exploration of Christian Community*. Harper One, 1954.

Boyd, Brady. Speaking Life: Words That Work Wonders*. David C Cook, 2020.

Hybels, Bill. Just Walk Across the Room: Simple Steps Pointing People to Faith*. Zondervan, 2006.

The Holy Bible, New International Version. Biblica, 2011.

The Holy Bible, New Living Translation. Tyndale House Publishers, 2015.

Ury, William. The Power of a Positive No: How to Say No and Still Get to Yes*. Bantam Books, 2007.

Wolgemuth, Nancy DeMoss. Encourage One Another*. Moody Publishers, 2020.

Inspired to Encourage
Appendices

Discussion Questions for Reflection or Small Groups

Chapter 1: The Foundations of Encouragement
1. What does biblical encouragement look like, and how does it differ from the world's view of encouragement?
2. How have you experienced encouragement within the Christian community? Share a specific instance.
3. Discuss the role of encouragement in spiritual growth. Can you think of a time when encouragement helped you grow in your faith?

Chapter 2: The Art of Saying No Positively
1. Why is it important for Christians to learn how to say "no" positively? Share an example from your own life.
2. How can saying "no" be an act of encouragement for both the giver and the receiver?
3. Reflect on when you had to set boundaries to maintain your spiritual health or relationships. How did it impact you and others?

Chapter 3: Building Bridges Through Encouragement
1. How can simple acts of kindness and conversation serve as bridges of encouragement to others?
2. Share a story where a small gesture made a big difference in your or someone else's life.
3. In what ways can we be more intentional about encouraging others in our daily interactions?

Chapter 4: The Encouragement of Community
1. Why is community essential for encouragement? Discuss how community has played a role in your spiritual life.
2. How can we foster an environment of encouragement within our communities?
3. Share an experience where the community helped you through a difficult time.

Chapter 5: The Power of Words
1. Discuss the impact of words as both a tool for encouragement and potential harm. How does this align with James 3:5-10?
2. Can you recall when someone's words deeply encouraged you? How did it affect your actions or beliefs?

3. How can we become more mindful of our words to ensure they encourage and uplift others?

Chapter 6: The Practice of Gratitude as Encouragement
1. Why is gratitude fundamental to encouragement? Share how expressing or receiving gratitude has encouraged you.
2. Discuss practical ways to cultivate gratitude in your life.
3. How can gratitude change our perspective during challenging times?

Chapter 7: Reflection as a Tool for Encouragement
1. How does reflection contribute to encouragement? Share how personal or communal reflection has impacted your faith journey.
2. Discuss the importance of reflective listening in encouraging others. Have you ever experienced a moment when being listened to felt particularly encouraging?
3. Reflect on a challenging situation. In hindsight, how did it encourage growth in your spiritual life or relationships?

Chapter 8: Encouragement in Leadership
1. What qualities make a leader effective at encouraging others? Share examples of encouraging leadership you have witnessed.
2. How can leaders balance the responsibility of directing with the need to encourage and uplift their team or congregation?
3. Discuss ways you can lead by encouragement in your spheres of influence, regardless of your official title or role.

These discussion questions are designed to spark deep conversation and personal reflection, helping group members and individuals explore and apply the book's themes to their lives. Encourage honesty, openness, and vulnerability for meaningful engagement and growth.

Living in Community
The New Testament's
"One Another" Passages

Love One Another
- *"A new command I give you: Love one another. As I have loved you, so you must love one another."* (John 13:34)

- *"My command is this: Love each other as I have loved you."* (John 15:12)

- *"This is my command: Love each other."* (John 15:17)

- *"Let no debt remain outstanding, except the continuing debt to love one another, for whoever loves others has fulfilled the law."* (Romans 13:8)

- *"Now about your love for one another we do not need to write to you, for you yourselves have been taught by God to love each other."* (1 Thessalonians 4:9)

- *"May the Lord make your love increase and overflow for each other and for everyone else, just as ours does for you."* (1 Thessalonians 3:12)

- *"Now that you have purified yourselves by obeying the truth so that you have sincere love for each other, love one another deeply, from the heart."* (1 Peter 1:22)

- *"Above all, love each other deeply, because love covers over a multitude of sins."* (1 Peter 4:8)

- *"And this is his command: to believe in the name of his Son, Jesus Christ, and to love one another as he commanded us."* (1 John 3:23)

- *"And now, dear lady, I am not writing you a new command but one we have had from the beginning. I ask that we love one another."* (2 John 1:5)

Bear One Another's Burdens
- *"Carry each other's burdens, and in this way you will fulfill the law of Christ."* (Galatians 6:2)

Greet One Another
- *"Greet one another with a holy kiss. All the churches of Christ send greetings."* (Romans 16:16)
- *"All the brothers and sisters here send you greetings. Greet one another with a holy kiss."* (1 Corinthians 16:20)
- *"Greet one another with a holy kiss."* (2 Corinthians 13:12)
- *"Greet one another with a kiss of love. Peace to all of you who are in Christ."* (1 Peter 5:14)

Be Kind and Compassionate
- *"Be kind and compassionate to one another, forgiving each other, just as in Christ God forgave you."* (Ephesians 4:32)
- *"Finally, all of you, be like-minded, be sympathetic, love one another, be compassionate and humble."* (1 Peter 3:8)

Do Good to Each Other
- *"Therefore, as we have opportunity, let us do good to all people, especially to those who belong to the family of believers."* (Galatians 6:10)
- *"Make sure that nobody pays back wrong for wrong, but always strive to do what is good for each other and for everyone else."* (1 Thessalonians 5:15)

Be Humble Towards One Another
- *"Do nothing out of selfish ambition or vain conceit. Rather, in humility value others above yourselves."* (Philippians 2:3)

Forgive Each Other
- *"Bear with each other and forgive one another if any of you has a grievance against someone. Forgive as the Lord forgave you."* (Colossians 3:13)

Encourage One Another
- *"That you and I may be mutually encouraged by each other's faith."* (Romans 1:12)

- *"Therefore encourage one another with these words."* (1 Thessalonians 4:18)

- *"Therefore encourage one another and build each other up, just as in fact you are doing."* (1 Thessalonians 5:11)

- *"But encourage one another daily, as long as it is called "Today," so that none of you may be hardened by sin's deceitfulness."* (Hebrews 3:13)

- *"And let us consider how we may spur one another on toward love and good deeds, not giving up meeting together, as some are in the habit of doing, but encouraging one another—and all the more as you see the Day approaching."* (Hebrews 10:24-25)

Build Up/Edify One Another
- *"Let us therefore make every effort to do what leads to peace and to mutual edification."* (Romans 14:19)

- *"Each of us should please our neighbors for their good, to build them up."* (Romans 15:2)

- *"Therefore encourage one another and build each other up, just as in fact you are doing."* (1 Thessalonians 5:11)

- *"Do not let any unwholesome talk come out of your mouths, but only what is helpful for building others up according to their needs, that it may benefit those who listen."* (Ephesians 4:29)

Serve One Another
- *"You, my brothers and sisters, were called to be free. But do not use your freedom to indulge the flesh; rather, serve one another humbly in love."* (Galatians 5:13)

Live in Peace and Harmony
- *"Live in harmony with one another. Do not be proud, but be willing to associate with people of low position. Do not be conceited."* (Romans 12:16)

- *"But if the unbeliever leaves, let it be so. The brother or the sister is not bound in such circumstances; God has called us to live in peace."* (1 Corinthians 7:15)

- *"Finally, brothers and sisters, rejoice! Strive for full restoration, encourage one another, be of one mind, live in peace. And the God of love and peace will be with you."* (2 Corinthians 13:11)

These verses are in the New International Version (NIV) translation.

30-Day Encouragement Challenge

Day 1: Send an Encouraging Text
Reach out to a friend or family member with a text message that offers encouragement or expresses appreciation.

Day 2: Leave a Positive Note
Write a positive note and leave it somewhere for a loved one or even a stranger to find.

Day 3: Compliment Someone Genuinely
Give a sincere compliment to someone in your life, whether a coworker, friend, or family member.

Day 4: Share an Uplifting Quote or Scripture
Post an uplifting quote or Scripture on your social media, or send it directly to someone who might need it.

Day 5: Listen Actively
Always listen actively to someone without interrupting or offering advice, just being present for them.

Day 6: Offer to Help
Offer help to someone who could use it, whether running errands, doing chores, or assisting with a project.

Day 7: Pray for Someone
Pray for someone and let them know they were in your prayers today.

Day 8: Encourage Someone's Dream
Encourage someone to pursue a dream or goal they've shared with you, affirming your belief in their capability.

Day 9: Gratitude Call
Call someone to express your gratitude for their presence in your life simply.

Day 10: Write an Encouraging Letter
Write a letter or email to someone, highlighting their strengths and positive impact on you or others.

Day 11: Give a Small Gift
Give someone a small, thoughtful gift to show that you're thinking of them.

Day 12: Offer a Word of Affirmation
Affirm someone's efforts, progress, or character in a specific way.

Day 13: Share a Meal
Share a meal with someone and use the time to uplift and encourage one another.

Day 14: Create an Encouragement Jar
Start an encouragement jar, filling it with positive notes for someone to draw from whenever they need a boost.

Day 15: Support a Local Business and Spread Positivity
Support a local business with your patronage and leave a positive review to encourage their hard work.

Day 16: Encourage Self-Care
Encourage someone to take time for self-care, even if it's just reminding them to take a break or enjoy a hobby.

Day 17: Celebrate an Achievement
Celebrate someone's achievement, big or small, with a message, call, or small gathering.

Day 18: Be a Cheerleader for Someone's Efforts
Actively cheer someone on as they work toward a goal, offering your support and enthusiasm.

Day 19: Host a Positivity Night
Host a gathering (virtual or in-person) dedicated to sharing positive stories, gratitude, and encouragement.

Day 20: Promote Someone's Work or Project
Promote a friend or acquaintance's work, project, or business on social media to show support.

Day 21: Volunteer Your Time
Volunteer for a cause someone cares about to support and encourage their passion.

Day 22: Send an Encouraging Book or Article
Send someone a book or article you found inspiring, encouraging them to read it.

Day 23: Acknowledge Personal Growth
Acknowledge and celebrate someone's personal growth, noting specific areas where you've seen them change or improve.

Day 24: Craft a Personalized Playlist
Create a personalized playlist of uplifting or meaningful songs for someone.

Day 25: Give a Token of Appreciation
Give someone a token of appreciation that symbolizes your gratitude or admiration.

Day 26: Share a Testimony
Share a personal testimony of encouragement, either one-on-one or in a small group, highlighting God's faithfulness.

Day 27: Encourage Someone to Keep Going
Reach out to someone who might be struggling and encourage them to keep going, offering your support.

Day 28: Post a Public Thank You
Post a public thank you or shout-out to someone who deserves recognition, doing so on social media or another public platform.

Day 29: Organize a Surprise of Encouragement
Organize a surprise for someone (like a video compilation of friends sharing encouraging words) to uplift their spirits.

Day 30: Reflect and Share Your Experience
Reflect on the past 30 days of encouragement. Share your experience with someone and encourage them to start their challenge.

This challenge is designed to foster a habit of kindness and support that radiates through your daily interactions, transforming the lives of those you encourage and enriching your spiritual journey.

Here's how to continue the momentum beyond the 30-day mark:

Extend the Challenge
Consider repeating the challenge, perhaps focusing on different people in your life or exploring new ways to encourage those around you. Encouragement can take many forms, and variety can keep your efforts fresh and impactful.

Reflect and Adjust
Take time to reflect on the impact of your actions, not just on others but on your growth and well-being. Identify the practices that were most meaningful to you and those you encouraged. Adjust your approach based on what you learn about yourself and the needs of your community.

Incorporate Encouragement into Your Routine
Make encouragement a natural part of your daily routine. This could mean setting aside time each morning to think of who you might encourage that day or creating regular reminders to reach out to others.

Encourage a Culture of Encouragement
Share the 30-day encouragement challenge concept with your church, small group, or community. Inspiring others to take up the challenge can amplify the positive effects, creating a culture of encouragement where everyone feels uplifted and valued.

Journal Your Journey
Keep a journal of your encouragement, efforts, and reflections. Writing down your experiences can provide insights into the power of encouragement and how it changes both the giver and the receiver. This can also serve as a personal reminder of God's work in your life by encouraging others.

Deepen Your Understanding
Continue to seek out resources on encouragement, whether through books, sermons, workshops, or podcasts. Learning from others can provide new ideas and deepen your understanding of what it means to live out biblical encouragement.

Pray for Guidance
Pray regularly for God to guide you to those who need encouragement. Ask for sensitivity to the Holy Spirit's prompting

so that you might be an instrument of God's love and comfort to those around you.

Set Long-Term Goals
Consider setting long-term goals for how you want to grow in the ministry of encouragement. This might involve specific relationships you want to strengthen, communities you want to impact, or personal qualities you wish to develop.

Evaluate and Celebrate
Periodically evaluate the impact of your encouragement on others and yourself. Celebrate the victories, no matter how small, and thank God for the opportunity to serve Him in this way. Recognizing the difference your encouragement makes can be a powerful motivator to continue.

The journey of encouragement is a lifelong pursuit that enriches our walk with God and deepens our connections with others. By continuing to practice and prioritize encouragement, you contribute to a legacy of love that reflects the heart of Christ to the world.

Scripture Reference Guide for Encouragement

This guide compiles a selection of Bible verses centered around themes of encouragement, comfort, hope, and love. Whether you need a word of upliftment or seek to encourage someone else, these verses can serve as a powerful reminder of God's promises and faithfulness.

Encouragement
Isaiah 41:10
Don't be afraid, for I am with you. Don't be discouraged, for I am your God. I will strengthen you and help you. I will hold you up with my victorious right hand.

Joshua 1:9
This is my command—be strong and courageous! Do not be afraid or discouraged. For the Lord your God is with you wherever you go.

1 Thessalonians 5:11
So encourage each other and build each other up, just as you are already doing.

Comfort
2 Corinthians 1:3-4
All praise to God, the Father of our Lord Jesus Christ. God is our merciful Father and the source of all comfort. He comforts us in all our troubles so that we can comfort others. When they are troubled, we will be able to give them the same comfort God has given us.

Psalm 23:4
Even when I walk through the darkest valley, I will not be afraid, for you are close beside me. Your rod and your staff protect and comfort me.

Matthew 5:4
God blesses those who mourn, for they will be comforted.

Hope
Romans 15:13
I pray that God, the source of hope, will fill you completely with joy and peace because you trust in him. Then you will overflow with confident hope through the power of the Holy Spirit.

Exploring Encouragement in Christian Community

Hebrews 11:1
Faith shows the reality of what we hope for; it is the evidence of things we cannot see.

Jeremiah 29:11
For I know the plans I have for you," says the Lord. "They are plans for good and not for disaster, to give you a future and a hope.

Love
1 Corinthians 13:4-7
Love is patient and kind. Love is not jealous or boastful or proud or rude. It does not demand its own way. It is not irritable, and it keeps no record of being wronged. It does not rejoice about injustice but rejoices whenever the truth wins out. Love never gives up, never loses faith, is always hopeful, and endures through every circumstance.

1 John 4:16
We know how much God loves us, and we have put our trust in his love. God is love, and all who live in love live in God, and God lives in them.

Romans 8:38-39
And I am convinced that nothing can ever separate us from God's love. Neither death nor life, neither angels nor demons, neither our fears for today nor our worries about tomorrow—not even the powers of hell can separate us from God's love. No power in the sky above or in the earth below—indeed, nothing in all creation will ever be able to separate us from the love of God that is revealed in Christ Jesus our Lord.

This collection of scriptures is a treasure trove of God's promises and character, designed to lift spirits, bolster faith, and remind us of the profound love and hope we have in Christ. Whether for personal meditation or as words of encouragement to share, let these verses be a source of strength and comfort. (These verses are in the New Living Translation—NLT translation.)

Guide to Active Listening

Active listening is a skill that enhances communication, fosters understanding and deepens relationships. It involves fully concentrating, understanding, responding, and remembering what is said. Here are practical tips and exercises to become an effective active listener, particularly in providing encouragement and support.

Principles of Active Listening
1. **Give Full Attention**: Turn off or put away distractions. Make eye contact (if culturally appropriate) and turn your body towards the speaker, showing you are fully engaged.

2. **Show That You're Listening**: Use non-verbal cues such as nodding, smiling, and other facial expressions or verbal sounds like "mm-hmm" or "I see" to indicate that you are actively listening.

3. **Provide Feedback**: Reflect on what has been said by paraphrasing. "So, what you're saying is..." or "It sounds like you feel..." are great ways to show that you are processing the information shared.

4. **Defer Judgment**: Allow the speaker to finish their thoughts before forming a judgment or offering advice. Active listening involves understanding the speaker's perspective, even if you disagree.

5. **Respond Appropriately**: Active listening is an opportunity to encourage and support. Offer appropriate responses that acknowledge the speaker's feelings and perspectives.

Exercises to Enhance Active Listening Skills

1. **The Paraphrase Exercise**
    - Objective: To practice expressing what the speaker is saying in your own words.
    - How to Do It: Periodically summarize what the other person has said in a conversation. Ask for confirmation to ensure your interpretation is accurate. This helps in better understanding and shows the speaker they are being heard.

2. **The Reflection Exercise**
   - Objective: To practice acknowledging the feelings behind the speaker's words.
   - How to Do It: Identify the emotions you believe the speaker is experiencing and reflect them, e.g., "It seems like you're passionate about this" or "You sound relieved." This validates their feelings and encourages deeper sharing.

3. **The Question-Asking Exercise**
   - Objective: To encourage deeper insights and sharing without steering the conversation.
   - How to Do It: Ask open-ended questions that prompt further explanation or thought, such as "What happened next?" or "How did that make you feel?" Avoid leading or closed questions that can be answered with a simple "yes" or "no."

4. **The Distraction Elimination Exercise**
   - Objective: To improve concentration on the speaker without external or internal distractions.
   - How to Do It: Practice listening in environments with different noise levels. Challenge yourself to focus on the speaker regardless of interruptions or background noise. At home, practice listening without checking your phone or engaging in other activities.

5. **The Empathy Building Exercise**
   - Objective: To develop a deeper understanding and empathy towards others' perspectives.
   - How to Do It: Engage in conversations to learn as much as possible about the other person's point of view. Afterward, reflect on how learning their perspective has affected your understanding of their situation.

Tips for Encouraging Others Through Active Listening
- **Affirm the Speaker**: Use encouraging phrases like "I'm glad you shared that with me" or "It sounds like you've been through a lot" to affirm and validate their sharing.
- **Offer Support**: After listening, ask how you can support them. Sometimes, offering your presence and continued listening is the best support.

- **Follow Up**: Demonstrate the lasting impact of your listening by referencing previous conversations and inquiring about developments or feelings since then.

Active listening encourages those who share with you and enriches your understanding and compassion, building more robust, meaningful relationships.

Prayer Guide for Encouragement

Prayer is a powerful tool for seeking and providing encouragement. Through prayer, we can draw near to God, laying our burdens at His feet and interceding on behalf of others. This guide offers a framework for praying for encouragement, including scriptural prayers and templates to help you pray more effectively for yourself and others needing encouragement.

Praying for Yourself
When seeking encouragement for yourself, it's important to remember that God is your source of strength and comfort. Here are ways to pray for personal encouragement:

1. **Acknowledge Your Need**: Start by honestly expressing your discouragement, fear, or weakness to God. He cares deeply about every aspect of your life.

2. **Seek God's Presence**: Ask God to make His presence known to you, comforting and reassuring you of His love and care.

3. **Claim God's Promises**: Recite and claim promises from Scripture that speak to God's faithfulness and your identity in Him.

Example Prayer:
"Heavenly Father, I come before You feeling [express your feelings]. I ask for Your comfort and strength to fill my heart. Remind me of Your promises in Scripture, such as [mention any specific promise or verse that speaks to you], and help me to trust in Your faithfulness. Encourage my spirit today, Lord, and renew my hope. In Jesus' name, Amen."

Praying for Others
Interceding for others is a powerful act of love. When praying for someone else's encouragement, consider these steps:

1. **Lift Them Up**: Begin by lifting the person's name before God, asking Him to bless and watch over them.

2. **Ask for Specific Needs**: If you're aware of specific

challenges they're facing, ask God to meet those needs, whether for peace, strength, wisdom, or comfort.
3. **Pray for God's Presence**: Ask God to make His presence felt in their life, providing assurance and hope.

Example Prayer:
"Lord God, I lift [name] to You today. They are facing [describe the situation], and I ask that You provide them with the strength and peace they need. Surround them with Your love, and remind them of Your never-failing presence. May they feel Your encouragement today as You guide them through this challenge. Equip me to be a source of support for them. In Jesus' name, Amen."

Scriptural Prayers for Encouragement
Using Scripture as the foundation of your prayers can be incredibly powerful. Here are a couple of examples:

For Strength and Courage:
"Lord, Your Word says in Joshua 1:9 to 'be strong and courageous.' I pray for [name/self] to experience Your strength and courage in every aspect of life. May Your peace guard their heart and mind."

For Hope and Renewal:
"Father, according to Romans 15:13, You are the God of hope. Fill [name/self] with all joy and peace as they trust in You so they may overflow with hope by the power of the Holy Spirit."

Creating Personalized Prayers
When crafting your prayers, it can be helpful to:
1. **Start with Scripture**: Choose a verse that speaks to the situation or need.
2. **Be Specific**: Tailor your prayer to address specific needs, feelings, or circumstances.
3. **Speak from the Heart**: Your prayer doesn't have to be eloquent; it should just be sincere.

Template
"Dear God, I come to You for [specific need]. Your Word in [Scripture reference] promises [what the Scripture says], and I hold onto that promise now. I ask for Your [specific request] and thank You for Your faithfulness. Help me to see Your hand at work in my life. Amen."

Exploring Encouragement in Christian Community

This prayer guide is designed to be a starting point. Feel free to adapt and personalize your prayers to fit the unique circumstances you or others are facing. Remember, the most powerful prayers are those offered with a sincere heart and a steadfast faith in God's promises.

Praying for Global Concerns

Praying for global concerns broadens our perspective and deepens our compassion for the needs beyond our immediate surroundings. It reminds us of our interconnectedness and the power of God to work across the vastness of our world. Here's how to include global concerns in your prayer life with examples.

Understanding Global Concerns

Global concerns encompass a wide range of issues, including but not limited to:
- Natural disasters (earthquakes, hurricanes, floods)
- Humanitarian crises (refugee displacement, famine, poverty)
- Health pandemics
- Conflicts and wars
- Persecution of Christians and other religious or ethnic groups

Praying for Global Concerns

1. **Stay Informed:** Keep abreast of global events and issues through reliable news sources or humanitarian organizations. Understanding the context helps you pray more specifically and insightfully.
2. **Seek God's Heart**: Ask God to give you His heart and compassion for the people and situations affected by global issues. Pray for guidance on how to respond or contribute beyond prayer.
3. **Pray for Immediate Needs**: Pray for the immediate relief of those affected by crises, such as safety, health, food, and shelter.
4. **Pray for Long-Term Solutions**: Seek God's wisdom and intervention in resolving underlying issues causing or exacerbating the crises.
5. **Pray for Leaders and Decision-Makers**: Intercede for wisdom, compassion, and righteous action for leaders and organizations responding to these issues.
6. **Pray for the Church's Response**: Ask God to mobilize His

church worldwide to provide hope, aid, and the gospel's light amid these challenges.

Example Prayers for Global Concerns

For Natural Disasters
"Father God, we bring those affected by the recent [specific disaster] before You. Provide comfort to those grieving, strength to the rescue teams, and provision for all immediate needs. Guide the efforts of aid organizations and governments to respond effectively. Stir Your church to act in compassion and support. Amen."

For Humanitarian Crises
"Lord of mercy, we pray for the millions displaced by war, famine, and persecution. Protect them, meet their physical needs, and offer hope in their despair. Inspire the global community to respond generously. Empower leaders with solutions that promote peace and restore dignity. Amen."

For Health Pandemics
"Heavenly Father, in the face of this global health crisis, we ask for Your healing hand over the sick and protection for the vulnerable—guide researchers in developing effective treatments and vaccines. Equip healthcare workers with strength and resilience. Help nations collaborate to overcome this challenge. Amen."

Broadening Your Prayer Perspective
Incorporating global concerns into your prayer life not only has the potential to impact those you pray for but also transforms your own heart. It cultivates a spirit of empathy, unity, and a deeper understanding of God's sovereignty over all the earth. As you pray for the world, you join a chorus of voices seeking God's grace and intervention across the nations.

Incorporating Encouragement into Daily Life

This template is designed to help you intentionally incorporate acts of encouragement into your daily routine. By setting specific, measurable, achievable, relevant, and time-bound (SMART) goals, you can make a tangible impact on those around you and cultivate a habit of encouragement.

Step 1: Reflect on Your Encouragement Goals
- Goal Statement: Define what you hope to achieve with your encouragement efforts. For example, "I want to uplift and support my family and friends through regular encouragement."

Step 2: Identify Specific Actions
- Daily Actions: List specific actions you can take to encourage others. For instance, "Send a motivational text to a friend" or "Leave a positive note for a family member."
- Weekly Actions: Identify actions you can take weekly to offer encouragement. For example, "Write an encouraging letter or email to someone different each week."

Step 3: Make Your Goals SMART
- Specific: Define who you will encourage and how. E.g., "Encourage my coworker by acknowledging their hard work on a project."
- Measurable: Determine how you'll measure your goal. E.g., "Send three encouraging messages per week."
- Achievable: Ensure your goal is realistic given your current commitments.
- Relevant: Choose goals that are meaningful to you and the recipient.
- Time-Bound: Set a timeframe for your goal. E.g., "Over the next month, I will..."

Step 4: Plan for Challenges
- Anticipate Obstacles: Think about potential challenges to meeting your encouragement goals and plan for how to address them.
- Flexibility: Be prepared to adjust your plan as needed. Life is unpredictable, and flexibility will help you stay committed to your encouragement goals.

Step 5: Track Your Progress
- Tracking Method: Decide how you will track your progress (e.g., journal, spreadsheet, app) and make a habit of regular updates.
- Reflection: Set aside time weekly or monthly to reflect on your progress, your encouragement's impact on others, and any adjustments needed to improve.

Step 6: Celebrate Successes
- Acknowledgment: Recognize your efforts and successes, no matter how small. Celebrating these moments can motivate you to continue.
- Share Your Experience: Consider sharing your journey with others. Your story can inspire and encourage them to spread positivity in their circles.

Action Plan Example
- Goal Statement: Strengthen my relationships by encouraging my friends and family actively.
- Actions
    - Daily: Send a text message to a friend or family member with a word of encouragement.
    - Weekly: Write an encouraging letter or email to someone needing a boost.
- SMART Goal: Over the next 30 days, I will send a daily encouragement text to different people and write four encouraging letters or emails.
- Challenges and Solutions: A potential challenge might be forgetting to send a daily text. To address this, I will set a daily reminder on my phone.
- Tracking: I will keep a journal of whom I've encouraged and any responses or outcomes I observe.
- Reflection: Every Sunday night, I will review my journal entries to reflect on the impact of my encouragement and adjust my actions for the following week.
- Celebration: After one month, I will celebrate my commitment to this goal by sharing my experience with my small group and encouraging them to join me in spreading encouragement.

This template is a starting point. Feel free to adapt it to fit your personal goals and lifestyle, ensuring it helps you weave encouragement into your daily life's fabric effectively.

Inventory of Spiritual Gifts

This inventory is designed to help you discover and understand your spiritual gifts. By identifying your gifts, you can explore ways to use them to encourage and serve others in your community. Answer the questions honestly and reflect on your experiences and inclinations. Remember, every gift is significant and serves a unique purpose in the body of Christ.

Instructions
For each statement below, rate yourself on a scale from 1 to 5, where:

1 = Rarely/Not at all, **2** = Occasionally, **3** = Sometimes, **4** = Often, **5** = Always/Almost Always

Questionnaire
1. I feel deeply moved to help others, often putting their needs above mine. Rating: _____

2. I find trusting God's promises easy and fulfilling, even under challenging circumstances. Rating: _____

3. Others often seek my advice or counsel when facing important decisions. Rating: _____

4. I am drawn to and enjoy studying and sharing the teachings of the Bible. Rating: _____

5. I am passionate about maintaining unity and peace within my community. Rating: _____

6. I often notice and take action to meet practical needs within my church or community. Rating: _____

7. I enjoy leading and organizing activities that promote spiritual growth.
Rating: _____

8. I feel compelled to share the message of Christ with those who do not know Him. Rating: _____

9. Praying for others is a priority, and I diligently intercede for them. Rating: _____

10. I am sensitive to the emotions and spiritual conditions of the people around me. Rating: _____

11. I find joy and satisfaction in generously supporting the church's mission. Rating: _____

12. I feel a strong sense of responsibility to protect and defend the truth of the Gospel. Rating: _____

13. I am knowledgeable about learning and understanding foreign languages and facilitating communication. Rating: _____

14. I often receive insights or understandings from God that bring clarity and direction. Rating: _____

15. Creating art, music, or other forms of creative expression is a way I connect with and serve God. Rating: _____

Scoring
- 65-75 Points: You may have leadership-oriented solid gifts (e.g., leadership, administration, teaching).
- 50-64 Points: Your gifts likely lean towards relational and nurturing roles (e.g., mercy, encouragement, pastoring).
- 35-49 Points: You might find your strengths in supportive and behind-the-scenes roles (e.g., service, giving, helps).
- Below 35: You may have gifts uniquely tailored to specific needs or times (e.g., wisdom, knowledge, faith).

Using Your Gifts to Encourage Others
- **Service/Helps**: Volunteer for tasks within your community or church, offering your time and skills to support others.
- **Teaching**: Lead a small group study or share Bible insights with those seeking to learn.
- **Encouragement**: Regularly reach out to others with words of comfort, hope, and affirmation.
- **Giving**: Find opportunities to support others or church initiatives financially or through donations.
- **Leadership**: Take initiative in organizing events or ministries that meet your community's spiritual or physical needs.
- **Mercy**: Be present for those in emotional distress, offering a listening ear and compassionate heart.
- **Wisdom/Knowledge**: To those facing decisions or

challenges, grounded in biblical truth, provide counsel and direction.
- **Faith**: Share your trust in God's promises, inspiring others to rely on Him in all circumstances.
- **Intercession**: Commit to praying for specific people or situations, interceding on behalf of those in need.
- **Evangelism**: Share the gospel with clarity and passion, inviting others to explore a relationship with Christ.

Remember, the purpose of your gifts is to serve others and glorify God. As you grow in your understanding and exercise of your spiritual gifts, remain open to the Holy Spirit's leading on how best to use them in your current context.

Echoes of Grace: The Art of Encouraging

In the garden of the spirit, where love's seeds gently lay,
There's a calling, soft and tender, in the light of day.
To uplift the weary hearts, to light the shadowed path,
Encouragement's a gift, a divine and sacred craft.

With words that dance like sunlight, or a touch that whispers grace,
A listener's ear, a shoulder, in the quiet, sacred space.
It's in the act of giving, we find ourselves receive,
The joy of being present, to love, to heal, to believe.

In the echoes of our actions, in the silence of our stance,
We mirror Christ's own love, in every glance.
For in the smallest gestures, a mighty love is shown,
Through encouragement we reveal the heart of God, made known.

It's not just in the grandeur, but in the quiet moments too,
A text, a note, a prayer, letting His light shine through.
So let us walk together, in encouragement's embrace,
Building bridges, lifting spirits, a community of grace.

As we practice this high calling, our hearts and souls entwine,
In the art of encouraging, we see the divine.
For every act of kindness, in every word of cheer,
We echo God's own voice, to those we hold dear.

*"Kind words can be
short and easy to speak,
but their echoes are truly endless."*

—Mother Teresa

Manufactured by Amazon.ca
Acheson, AB